Henry E. Seaton

The Flora of Mt. Orizaba

Henry E. Seaton

The Flora of Mt. Orizaba

ISBN/EAN: 9783337426903

Printed in Europe, USA, Canada, Australia, Japan

Cover: Foto ©Andreas Hilbeck / pixelio.de

More available books at **www.hansebooks.com**

The following notes and report are based upon a collection of plants made on Mt. Orizaba by the writer while Botanist of the J. T. Scovell expedition during July and August, 1891.

The first collections on Mt. Orizaba to which there is any scientific reference were made by Frederick Liebmann in 1841. He describes the volcano as the most remarkable mountain in North America. It has a latitude of 18° and lies surrounded by the very fertile country of Southern Mexico. It is only 90 miles from the gulf and having such a situation, there is presented upon its Eastern slope every phase of vegetation from tropical to alpine.

The regions in the vicinity of Cordoba and Orizaba at elevations of 3000° and 4000° and distances of sixty

among the families that made up the shrubby
& herbaceous flora were the Malvaceae Legumin-
moseae, Cucurbitaceae Rubiaceae, Compositae, Asclepiadaceae, Convolvulaceae, Solanaceae,
Euphorbiaceae and Commelinaceae besides
the grasses, sedges and ferns. In the
vicinity of Orizaba, the Compositae had
their greatest display. The essentially
American Helianthoideae were the forms most
abundant and not only are they characteristic
of this particular region but have in Mexico
their greatest concentration, amounting it has
been estimated to 32% of the species and 2/5
of the genera of all the Compositae of the
country. The suborder Eupatorieae ranks second in numerical strength, the genera Eupatorium & Stevia however containing nearly
all the species. The Asteroideae had but
little representation in the forms that
are so characteristic of the north, — Solidago,
Aster and Erigeron. All the other
suborders of Compositae were present,
excepting the Arctotideae and Calendulaceae
which are confined to Africa and the Mediterra-

were made by the writer but several species extend their range a few hundred feet higher and Dr. J. secured a Draba at 15,000°. The — is a list of the species as they have been deter. and at the close a synopsis the des. of the f. g. & sp.

and this zone of 5000° may be considered as the temperate region and that above 9000° as alpine   Many plants of the sub tropical region extended their range to the temperate and even to the alpine district. this being especially true of low growing plants like Oxalis, Stellaria Trifolium and several of the Malvas.

The temperate zone between 4000° and 9000° is characterized nevertheless by many genera & families that are not present or are hardly noticeable in the more tropical regions.   The genus Salvia and order Lythraceæ have an especially large distribution   Of the latter, Cuphea is the most important element, growing in great abundance under all conditions of soil & moisture   There are many representations from the Geraniaceæ, Borragineæ, Scrophularineæ, Verbenaceæ, ~~Bignoni-aceæ~~ Acanthaceæ and Amarantaceæ which

Compositae are Stevia, Achillea, Dahlia and Tagetes and besides Eupatorium and Baccharis the shrubby flora is represented by Rubus and Symphoricarpus. Prominent among the grasses are Bromus, Festuca, Agrostis, Triodia, Poa & Muehlenbergia and the ferns are represented by Asplenium, Adiantum, Cheilanthes & Woodsia.

At 11 000' – 12 000', the forests are entirely of pines & spruce. The greater part of the herbaceous flora at this alt. is made up of Pentstemon, Halenia, Cerastium, Acaena, Eryngium, Aracacia, Cnicus, Lupinus & Stenanthium.

At 13 000', the vegetation consists principally of Nasturtium, Cerastium, Arenaria, Potentilla, Phacelia, Castilleia & Lithospermum. The pine woods beginning at 7000' disappear at 13 000', excepting stunted forms that continue to 14 000'. At 13,500' the vegetation becomes scantier and the slopes more sandy and beset with masses of sharp pointed black & gray rocks. The dry ground produces species of Draba, Gnaphalium, Senecio, Cnicus, Agrostis, Bromus & Asplenium.

Even at 14 000' on the higher slopes

The following notes a[re]
based upon a collection of
on Mt. Orizaba by the writ
anist of the J. T. Dowell ex[pedition dur]
ing July and August. 1[...]

(The first collec[tion]
Orizaba to which there is an[y]
reference, was made by [...]
mann in 1841 ✗ ~~the describe~~
of O is desc. by Lieb[...]
as the most interesting mou[ntain]
America. It has a latitud[e]
lies surrounded by the ver[y]
country of Southern Mexico
90 miles from the Gulf an[d]
compass
a situation, there is presen[t]
po
eastern slope every phase
from tropical to alpine.)

The regions
of Cordoba & Orizaba at eleva[tion]
and 4000 and distances of 6
from the coast were the
at which collections wer n[...]
that altitude the vegetation
cal Palm, coffee, bananna[s]
trees grow in abundanc[e]
& sugar cane attains a hi[gh]
cultivation. Prominent an[...]
lies that make up the sh[...]

-phorbiaceæ and Commelinaceæ besides
the grasses, sedges and ferns.) In the vicinity of Orizaba ~~the Compositæ~~ had
their greatest ~~display.~~ The essentially American Helianthodiæ were the forms most
abundant and not only are they characteristic of this particular region, but have
in Mexico their greatest concentration,
amounting it has estimated to 32% of
the species and 2/5 of the genera of all the
Compositæ of the country. The Sub Order
Eupatoriæ ranks second in numerical
strength, the genera Eupatorium & Sk
however, contributing nearly all the species.

The Asteroideæ had but little representation
in the forms that are so characteristic of
the North, — Solidago Aster & Erigeron. All
the other sub-orders of the family were present, excepting the Arctotideæ & Calendulaceæ
which are confined to Africa & the Mediterra-
nean region.

Collections were made at
three successively higher stations till
the altitude of 9000' was reached and this

region extend their range to the tempe-
ate and even to the alpine district, this
being especially true of low growing plants
like Oxalis, Stellaria, Trifolium and several of
the Malvas. The temperate zone is characterized nevertheless by many genera & families
that are not present or are hardly noticeable
in the more tropical regions. The
genus Salvia & Order Lythraceae have an especially large distribution. Of the latter Cuphea
is the most conspicuous element, growing in great abundance under all conditions of soil & moisture.
There are many representatives from the Gerania-
ceae, Borragineae, Scrophularineae, Verbenaceae
Acanthaceae & Amarantaceae which take the
place in a great measure of the Rubiaceae
Asclepiadaceae, Solaneae, Euphorbiaceae and Commel-
inae in the tropics.
                    Great & rapid changes are
experienced in the flora as the slopes are as-
cended above 9000', and there are well marked
zones for the distribution of the plants till
the limit of vegetation is reached. Between 9000'
and 10000', species of Sisymbrium, Lepidium, Geum
Gaura, Epilobium Oenothera, Krynitzkia, Mimulus,
Castilleia, Verbena, Silene, Gentiana and Chenopodium
are the most characteristic forms of the herbaceous
flora Prominent among the Compositae are Stevia
Achillea, Dahlia & Tagetes and besides Eupatorium
& Baccharis, the shrubby flora is represented by
Rubus, Symphoricarpus & Buddleia Prominent
among the grasses are Bromus, Festuca, Agrostis and
Muehlenbergia and the ferns are represented by

Asplenium, Adiantum, Cheilanthes and Woodsia

At 11,000° - 12000°, the forests a
entirely of pines & spruce. The greater part of
herbaceous flora at this altitude is made u
of Penstemon, Halenia, Cerastium, Acaena, Er
gium, Arracaria, Cnicus, Lupinus & Stevart

At 13,000°, the vegetation cons
principally of Nasturtium, Cerastium, Arenaria, Po.
tilla, Phacelia, Castilleia & Lithospermum. J.
pine woods beginning at 7000°, disappear.
13000° excepting stunted forms that continue to 14,0
At 13,500° the vegetation becomes scantier and s
slopes more sandy & beset with masses of shar
pointed black & grey rocks. The dry sandy soi
produces species of Draba, Gnaphalium, Sr
Cnicus, Agrostis, Bromus and Asplenium.

Even at 14000° on the higher s
just at the snow line, there exists quite a s
ied vegetation with species of Draba, Sisymbr
Gnaphalium, Cnicus, Asplenium & the grasses
the sandy plain below. This was the highe
point at which collections were made but
eral species extend their range a ~~a~~ hund
feet higher & Dr. Scavell secured a Draba at s

The following is a list of t
species as they have been determined and
the close is a synopsis of the distributio
the families, genera & species.

In the ~~~~ space

Ranunculaceae.

Thalictrum longistylum. DC. Along streams.
    Orizaba . 4000°. July 25.
Anemone Mexicana - HBK. Rocky woods near
    Maltrata - 5482°. Aug 16.
Ranunculus groides - HBK. Pine forests. Mt.
    Orizaba. 11000°. Aug 5
Ranunculus peruvianus - Pers. Mt. Orizaba.
    13000° - Aug 7.

Papavaraceae.

Argemone Mexicana - L. Common in open
    fields - Esperanza Aug 14. 8000°.

Cruciferae

   Nasturtium impatiens Ch & Scle.? Mt. O
       9000° - Aug 4.
   Thelypodium sp?. Mt. O. 11000°. Aug 5.
   Draba myosotidoides - Hms. Mt. O. 14000° - Aug
   Thelypodium sp? Mt. O. 10000° - Aug. 8.
   Sisymbrium canescens. Nutt. Mt. O. 14000°. Aug 7.
   Sisymbrium galeottianum. Tourn. Mt. O.
       9000°. Aug 4.
   Brassica sativa L. (Introduced) Common

Capparideàe

Gynandropsis speciosa - DC.

16   Cleome sp.?   Cordoba. 3000°. Aug. 20
17   Cleome sp.?   Cordoba 3000° Aug. 20.

Polygaleàe.

18   Polygala - n. sp.?   near acicularis - Nat. a
     sp. described from Chihuahua in. 86.

Beaumontia?   Mt. O. 9000°. Aug. 9.

19   Polygala   Cordoba 3000°. Aug 21.

Caryophylleae.

20   Silene laciniata Cav.   In shady rich ra-
     vines   Mt. O. 10000°. Aug 8.
21   Cerastium volcanicum. Schl. Mt. O. 12000° Aug
22   Cerastium sp?   Mt. O 11000°. Aug 6.
23   Cerastium sp?   Mt. O. 13000 Aug 7.
24   Stellaria prostrata - Bald. Climbing on
     rocks. Orizaba. 4000° July 29.
25   Stellaria nemorum. L. Cordoba, 3000° Aug 21
26   Arenaria alsinoides. Willd. Mt. O. 9000° Aug 6
27   Arenaria alsinoides. W (narrow leaves
     form) Orizaba - 4000°. July 31.

Arenaria decussata. Willd. Mt. O. 11000°. Aug 8

Arenaria sp.? Mt. O. 9000 Aug 8.

Drymaria anomala. Wat. 9000°. Aug 8.

(Not reported by Hemsley from Mex.)

Hypericineae.

Hypericum pauciflorum. HBK. Orizaba
4000°. July 30.

Malvaceae.

Malva borealis Wallm (Introduced) Orizaba.
4000°. July 29

Callirhoe — n.sp.? (C. involucrata the
only sp. reported) Mt O. 9000°. Aug 4.

Malvastrum tricuspidatum. Gay. Orizaba
4000°. July 23.

Anoda cristata Schl. Orizaba, 4000° July 29

Sida ulmifolia Cav. Nogales 4200 4°. Aug 4.

Sphaeralcea sp.? City of M. 7000° July 20.

Pavonia spinifex Willd — Common — Orizaba
4000° July 30

Pavonia typhalea Cav. Orizaba, 4000° July 30.

Malvaviscus grandiflorus — Orizaba & Nogales
4000° & 4204°. Aug 24. & Aug 13

Geraniaceae

Erodium cicutarium L. Her. Along the
railroad - Esperanza .8000°. Aug 15.
Oxalis corniculata L. Orizaba 4000° July 29
& Mt. O. 10000°. Aug 6.
Oxalis vespertilionis TG. Limestone
ledges. Mt. O. 9000°. Aug 8.
No Oxalis is reported by Hems. from Mt.

Rutaceae

Zanthoxylon sp?. Near City of M. 7000°
July 20.

Simarubaceae.

Picramnia sp?. Orizaba 4000°. July 30.

Lupinus Mexicanus. Cerv. Abundant
      in Pine forests. Mt.O.12000°. Aug 6.
Lupinus elegans. HBK. Mt.O.12000° Aug 6.
Lupinus sp?. Near Esperanza - on Rocky
      hills. 8000°. Aug 14.
Trifolium amabile. HBK. Mt.O.10000. Aug
Trifolium reflexum. L. (A very narrow
      leaved form.) Orizaba. 4000°. July 2
Medicago lupulina. L. (Introduced). Orizaba
      4000° July 20.
Eysenhardtia amorphoides HBK - Leaves &
      pods very long! Near Maltrata.
      5482°. Aug 16.
Dalea plumosa. Watson. n. var. 8000°Aug
Dalea sericea. Lag. - Both Daleas on
      rocky hills near Esperanza.
Indigofera mucronata. Spreng. Nogales.
      4202°. Aug -
Indigofera sp?. Orizaba 4000° July
Astragalus Helleri. Fenz Mt.O.9000°. Aug 8.
Desmodium orbiculare. Schlecht. Maltrata.

71 Phaseolus macropoides. Gray. ? Oriz. 4000°
72 Phaseolus sp?. Esperanza. 8000 - Aug 15
73 Rhynchosia longeracemosa. Mart & Gal.
   Orizaba. 4000° July
74 Rhynchosia sp? Mt. O. 9000° Aug 8.
75 Rhynchosia sp?. Esperanza. 8000° Aug 14.
76 Eriosema sp?. Mt. O. 9000° Aug 8
77 Sophora sp?. Cordoba. 3000° Aug 20.
78 Cassia chamaecrista L. ? Cors. 3000° Aug 21.
79 Cassia occidentalis L. Nogales. 4202°.
80 Cassia patellaria DC Oriz. 4000° July 31
81 Zornia diphylla Pers. Oriz. 4000°
82 Acacia farnesiana. Wills - Oriz 4000°
83 Acacia filicina. Wills - Oriz. 4000°.
84 Pithecolobium brevifolium. Benth. Esperanza.
   Rocky hills - 8000° Aug 15.

Rosaceàe
   tribolulis? — C & Serm
85 Rubus n. sp? Near the aqueduct.
   Mt. O. 10000° - Aug 8.
86 Rubus sp?. Found only in fruit. Mt. O.
   10000° Aug. 6.
87 Geum n. sp. nearest macrophyllum
   Mt. O. 10000° Aug 8.
88 Potentilla richardii Lehm? Mt. O. 13000° Aug 7.
89 Acaena elongata. L. Mt 12000°. Aug 6.

Crassulaceàe

90 Cotyledon sp² On shady Cliffs - Esperanza
91 Cotyledon sp²   8000° - Aug 14.

Melastomaceàe

92 Rhexia - sp². Cordaba. 3000° Aug 20
            Hemsley doubts the presence of R.
               in Mexico.
93 Heeria². sp². Cordaba, 3000° Aug 20.

Lythraceàe

94 Cuphea àequpetala, Cav. Esperanza, 8000°
95 Cuphea cyanea. DC². (Leaves scabrous!)
               Oriz. 4000°
96 Cuphea hysopifolia - NBK. Cordaba
               3000°. Aug 20.
97 Cuphea lanceolata. Ait. (Pedicels not de-
            flexed.) Oriz. 4000°
98 Cuphea Llavea - Llav. + Lex.   Oriz. 4000°
99 Cuphea Tolukana - Peyr.   Esperanza. 8000°.

101. Jussiaea peruviana – L. Orizaba. 4000°
Aug 13.

102. Jussiaea suffruticosa – L. Oriz. 4000° Aug.

103. Oenothera rosea – Ait. Common in
open fields. Oriz. 4000. July 29.

104. Oenothera sinuata, Mx. Mt. O. 10000° Aug 5

105. Oenothera ~~XXXX~~ Pine forests. Mt.
O. 11500°. Aug 6.

106. Lopezia mexicana – Jacq. Rocky hills
Orizaba 4000°. July 31.

107. Lopezia pumila HBK. Mt. O. 9000° Aug. 8.

108. Gaura coccinea – Nutt. Mt. Oriz.
9000°. Aug. 4.

Passifloraceae

109. Passiflora Mexicana Juss. Cordoba.
3000° - Aug. 20.

Cucurbitaceae

110. Melothria scabra – Naud. Mt. O. 9000°
Aug 4.

Umbelliferàe

Eryngium cymosum -Delar. Mt. O.
           10000°. Aug 5.

Eryngium protaeflorum -Delar. Mt. O.
           12000°. Aug. 6.

Sanicula mexicana. Dc. Orizaba. 4000°
           July 29.

Arracacia acuminata - Benth. Orizaba.
           4000°- July 30.

Apium leptophyllum F. Müll. Mt. O. 9000°
       Aug. 8. Reported for the first time
       from Mt. O.

Angelica mexicana. Vatke - Oriz. 4000° July 2,

Peucedanum sp? Mt. O. 10000°

Osmorrhiza brevistylis -DC. Mt. O.
           12000°- Aug. 6.

Daucus pusillus. Mx. Mt. O. 10000
       Aug. 6. Reported for the first
       time from Mt. O. the only station
       given in Hemsley being Chihuahua.

Arracacia sp? Mt. O. 9000°

Arracacia sp? Orizaba, 4000°-.

Rubiaceaè

125 Bouvardia triphylla - Sasili   Mt. O.
   Shady woods.   10,000°. Aug. 5.

126 Bouvardia qualenifolia. DC.   Mt. O. 10000°
   Shady Woods.   Aug.

127 Bouvardia leiantha. Benth.   Orizaba,
   Rocky hill   4000° - July 31.

128 Houstonia - n. sp? (Rocky hills) Orizaba,
   4000°. July 30

129 Crusea sp? Orizana 4000°. July 31

130 Crusea sp? Mt. O. 10,000° Aug. 6.

131 Crusea. sp?. Cordaba, 3000°. Aug. 21.

132 Spermacoce laevis. Lam.   Orizaba.
   4000° Aug 24.

133 Spermacoce parviflora. J.J.N.Mey. Cordaba,
   3000°. Aug 21

134 Richardsonia scabra, Ash.Kil. Cordaba,
   3000° Aug 21

135 Galium mexicanum - HBK. Orizaba,
   4000° - July 31.

136 Galium uncinulatum. DC. Orizaba. 4000° July 29

137 Galium - nearest uropetalum. Hems.   Mt. O.
   10,000° - Aug 5.

138 <u>Valerianeàe</u>

139 Valeriana mexicana - DC.   Mt. O. 9000° &
　　　　　　　　　　Maltrata . 5482° - Aug. 16.
140 Valeriana scandens - Linn.   Along roads.
　　　　　　　　　　Orizaba - 4000°. July 27

<u>Compositae</u>.

141 Piquieria trinervia - Cav.   Mt O. 9000°
　　　　　　　　　　　　　　Aug 8.
142 Ageratum Mexicanum - Sims   Orizaba.
　　　　　　　　　　4000° - July 26.
14_ Stevia conferta - DC. var puberula - DC (DC.
　　　　not Hems.) Mt. O. 9000° Aug 8.
143 Stevia elatior HBK.   Near Esperanza,
　　　　　　　　　8000° - Aug 14.
144 Stevia ovaefolia Willd - var. Bogotensis, D.C.
　　　　　　　　Near Nogales 4202°. Aug 13.
145 Stevia lucida - Lag.   Near Maltrata -
　　　　　Rocky hills . 5482° - Aug 16
146 Stevia salicifolia - Cav. Mt. O. 9000°. Aug 4.
147 Stevia trachelioides - DC. (Leaves t. mentose
　　　　　　　below.) Maltrata, 5482° Aug.
148 Eupatorium grandidentatum - DC. Mt. O.
　　　　　　　　　12000°. Aug 6"
149 Eupatorium populifolium - HBK.   Around
　　　　　fields - Orizaba 4000°. July 26.

10,000° - Aug. 5.

Erigeron canadensis - L. Common along deserted roads - Cordoba - 3,000° Aug 20.

Erigeron coronopifolius - Gray. Mt. O. 10,000° - Aug. 5.

Gnaphalium spicatum. Lam. Mt. O. 10,000°. Aug. 8.

Melampodium divaricatum - DC. Common in open fields. Orizaba 4000° July 2.

Melampodium oblongifolium - DC. Orizaba 4000° - Aug. 24.

Melampodium perfoliatum - HBK. Orizaba 4000° - July 27.

Parthenium hysterophorus - Linn. Orizaba 4000°. July 23.

Ambrosia artemisiaefolia - L. Common along the railroad. O. 4000° July 26.

Zinnia leptopoda - DC Multisata on a rocky hill 5482°. Aug. 15.

Heliopsis buphthalmoides. Dun. Common along railroad. Orizaba 4000°. Aug 24

Laluzania angusta. Schz. Bip. Mt O. along sides of cliffs. 9000° - Aug 9.

Sclerocarpus schiedeanus - B. & H. Orizaba.
4000° - July 23.

Tithonia diversifolia - Gray Not reported by
Hemsley. Orizaba. 4000° - Aug 24.

Viguiera canescens DC. Near Esperanza
8000°. Aug 15.

Viguiera, n sp? Woods near Esperanza
8000° Aug 15

Gymnolomia - sp? Woods near Esperanza.
8000° Aug 15.

Helianthus sp? Abundant in open fields.
Esperanza - 8000° Aug 14.

Melanthera deltoidea - Rich. Rather common
along the R.R. Orizaba, 4000° Aug.24

Actinomeris ovata. Nutt. Near Esperanza.
8000°. Aug 14.

Polymnia maculata. Cav. Orizaba - 4000°
Rocky hill. July 31.

Synedrella ualis - Gray - Orizaba. 4000° July 23
Not reported by Hems.

Dahlia coccinea - Cav. Orizaba. 4000° July 13.

Dahlia variabilis Desf. In shady ravines -
Mt. O. 10000° - Aug 8.

Galinsoga parviflora - Very Common in
roadsides - Orizaba. 4000° July 23

Dysodia chrysanthemoides - Lag. Along the
Vera Cruz R.R. near City of M. 7000°. July 20

4202° - Aug 13.

180 Tagetes . patula _ L.   Rocky hill . near Es-
            peranza . 8000° . aug 15

181 Chrysactinia mexicana _ Gray.   Rocky hill . near
            Esperanza - 8000'. aug 15

182 Achillea millaefolium _ L   Common on sandy
            plains near Esperanza . 8000° aug 15.

183 Senecio gerberaefolius _ Schz .   Mt . O.
                    13,500° aug 7.

184 Senecio procumbens _ HBK   Mt. O.
                    13,500°. aug 7.

185 Schistocarpha bicolor . Less.   Near Cordoba
                 3000° . aug 21.

186 Sonchus oleraceus . L. (Common as an intro-
            duced weed). Orizaba . 4000° July 20
            Esperanza - 8000° - Aug 14.

187 Pinaropappus roseus _ Less.   On limestone
            ledges _ Mt . O. 9000° _ aug 8,

Asclepias curassavica - L. Common in
open fields. Orizaba 4000° & Nogales. 4302°
Asclepias ovata . Mart. & Gal . Rocky Hill
Orizaba, 4000° July 31.
Gonolobus fraternus . Schl . Orizaba,
4000°. July.
Gonolobus gracilis . Dene. Rocky Hill.
Maltrata - 5482° - Aug 15.

caerulea – Don.

Loeselia – ⌖⌖ Mt O. 9000° – Aug. 9.

Hydrophyllaceàe

Phacelia *remaniuoides*, *lacu usp Jertle*
n. sp. Mt. O. 11500°. Aug.

Borragineàe.

Heliotropium Indicum – L. Cordoba 3000. Aug 2
Heliotropium limbatum – Bent. Grassy hills
near Malhata – 5482° – Aug. 16.
Krynitzkia angustifolium – Torr. Common at
10,000° Mt. O. Aug. 8.
Lithospermum distichum – Ort or spathulatum, M. G.
Grassy hills. Esperanza. 8000°. Aug 14.
Lithospermum strictum – Lehm. Esperanza. aug.
Lithospermum. sp? Mt. O. 13000°. Aug. 6.

Convolvulaceàe

Ipomaea sp? Orizaba 4000° Aug 24.
Ipomaea *stans – Cav.* Esperanza 8000° Aug 14.
Ipomaea sp? Mt. O. 9000° Aug 8.
Ipomaea sp? Cordoba 3000° Aug 21
Ipomaea sp? Cordoba 3000° Aug 21
Ipomaea sp? Orizaba 4000° July 25.
Ipomaea sp. Orizaba 4000° July 25
Ipomaea bona-nox – L. Orizaba July 20.

216 | Solanum nigrum. L. Mt. O. 9000°. Aug 5.
217 | Solanum rostratum Dun. Mt. O. 9000. Aug 5.
218 | Solanum tuberosum - L. Mt. O. 10.000 Aug 5.
219 | Solanum torvum - Sw. (very variable)
　　　　　　　　Near Cordaba. 3.000° Aug 20.
220 | Solanum amazonium. Ker - Cordaba,
　　　　　　　　　　3.000° Aug 20
221 | Solanum demissum. Lindl. Esperanza,
　　　　　　　　　　8.000° Aug 14.
222 | Solanum elaeagnifolium. Cav. Orizaba
　　　　　　　　　　4000° July 27.
223 | Solanum sp? Esperanza - Sandy fields. Aug 13.
224 | Physalis aequata - Jacq. Esperanza, 8000' Aug 1.
225 | Physalis Philadelphica, Lam. var. minor!.
　　　　　　　　Orizaba. 4000°.
　　　　　　　　Small form at Cordaba, 3000°.?
226 | Sarracha jaltomata Schl. Cordaba, 3000°. Aug 21.
227 | Datura arborea. L. Orizaba. 4000° July.
228 | Cestrum sp? (Common) Cordaba, 3000° Aug 2.
229 | Nicotiana - nearest Mexicana. Schl
　　　　　　　　Orizaba. 4000°. July 30.

Scrophularineàe.

aqueduct. 9000°. Aug 4.

235 Mimulus sp*. Esperanza. 8000°. Aug 14

236 Sibthorpia pichinchensis _ HBK. Mt. O.
10.000°. Aug. 6.

237 Veronica peregrina. L. ~~Wheat fields near~~
~~Esperanza~~ Mt. O. 10000° Aug 6.

238 Veronica agrestis L. (a naturalized sp. from the
old world). Wheat fields. Esperanza. Aug 14.

239 Buchnera pilosa. Benth. Orizaba. 4000°. July 31.

240 Castilleia lithospermoides HBK. Mt. O.
11.5000°. Aug. 6.

241 Castilleia integrifolia _ L. Mt. O. 9000°. Aug 4.

242 Lamourouxia cordata. Ch. & Schl. Esperanza;
8000° Aug 14. & Oriz. 4000° July 31.

243 Lamourouxia multifida _ HBK. Orizaba.
Rocky Hills _ 4000° _ July 31.

Orobanchaceàe

244 Pinguicula caudata. Schl. Shady
cliffs. Maltrata. 5482°. Aug. 16

Gesneraceàe

245 Anetanthus parviflorus. B. & H. Mt. O.
10.000°. Aug. 6.

Bignoniaceae.

246   Tecoma stans. Juss. var velutina. DC or
        n var.   Maltrata, 5482°. Aug 16.

Acanthaceae

247   Calophanes ovata. Benth - Fields near
            Nogales 4202°.

248   Calophanes schiedeana. Nees.   Hills near
            Maltrata. 5482° aug 15

249   Calophanes angustifolia - Nees. Hills
            near Orizaba - 4000° - July 31.

250   Ruella glandulosa - punctatus.   Hills west
            of Orizaba - 4000°. July 31

267 Verbena ciliata - Benth - Orizaba - July 23

268 Verbena teucriifolia. M. & G. Mt. O. 9000° Aug 9

269 Verbena n. sp.? Sandy hills near Esper- anza - 8000°, Aug 14.

270 Jamonea scabra - Ch & Schl. Along streams. Cordaba, 3000°. Aug 20.

271 Citharexylum reticulatum - HBK. Orizaba near a dwelling - 4000°. July 29.

Labiatae

272 Ocimum carnosum - L. & O. Orizaba - 4000°. July

273 Hyptis stellulata - Benth - Orizaba - 4000°. July

274 Hyptis spicata Pois - Orizaba - 4000°. July 25.

275 Micromeria brownei - Benth - Roadsides near Cordaba, 3000° - Aug 21.

276 Lepechinia spicata - Willd - Mt. O. 9000° - Aug 8.

277 Salvia angustifolia Cav Mt. O. 9000° Aug 8

278 Salvia grahami - Benth. Mt. O. 9000. Aug 8.

279 Salvia patens - Cav. Maltrata 5482°. Aug 13

280 Salvia tillaefolia. Vahl. Orizaba, 4000 July 26

281 Salvia ballotaeflora - Benth - Maltrata, Aug 15

282 Salvia amarissima - Ort. Near Esperanza, 8000° - Aug 14.

283 Salvia elegans - Vahl. Mt. O. 10000° Aug 8

284 Salvia hyptoides. M. & G. - Near Cordaba, 3000° Aug 20.

285 | Cedronella Mexicana – Benth? Mt. Ory.
In Ravines – 10,000°. Aug 8.

286 | Brunella vulgaris. L. Hills near Maltrata,
5482° – Aug 16.

287 | Marrubium vulgare. L. Mt. O. –
10,000°. Aug 8.

288 | ~~Stachys~~
Scutellaria caerulea – Moc. & Sesse.
Hills near Orizaba. 4000° July 31

289 | Stachys agraria – Ch. & Schl. Orizaba – July 29.

290 | Stachys coccinea – Jacq. Rocky hill near
Orizaba. 4000° July 31.

291 | Stachys Drummondii Benth – Orizaba. Aug 26

292 | Stachys repens – M. & G. ? Peak of O. 10,000°
Aug 6.

293 | Stachys – (§ 4. Genuinae & XII Sec – Cephalotyche)

294 | Teucrium inflatum Swz. near Orizaba
4000° July 29.

Plantagineàe

295 | Plantago major – L. Common in wet
places – Orizaba. 4000° July 29

296 | Plantago Virginica – L. Orizaba – July 29.
Plantago Xorullensis – HBK. Peak of
Orizaba. 11,000° Aug 6.

Nyctagineàe

298 Amarantus blitum — L.   Very common in
Oriaba 4000". July 23.

299 Gomphrena decumbens — Jacq.   Hills near
Maltrata. 4582° Aug 15

300 Gomphrena globosa — L.   Oriaba — July 29

301 Iresine gracilis — M. &G.   Oriaba — July 25

302 Iresine Hookeri . Mog.   Oriaba July 23.

Chenopodiaceàe

303 Chenopodium incisum — Poir   Peak of Oriaba.
10.000°. Aug 6.

304 Chenopodium foetidum — Schrad — Peak of O.
10.000° — Aug 6.

Phytolaccaceàe

305 Phytolaca octandra — L.   Nogales. 4202° Aug 13.

~~306~~ Polygonaceàe

306 Polygonum glabrum — Willd — Oriaba July 25

307 Polygonum hydropiperoides — Mx., Oriaba July 29

308 Polygonum nodosum, Pers.   Oriaba — July 23

309 Polygonum segetum — HBK   Near Cordoba
3000° Aug 20

310 Rumex crispus L. var. mexicanus M.G.
Peak of Oriaba — 9000° — Aug 4.

311 Rumex sp?   Esperanza, 5000°. Aug 15

Piperaceàe

312 Piper aduncum L.? Orizaba. 4000° July 30.

Euphorbiaceàe

313 Euphorbia graminea - Jacq. Oruzaba -
4000°. July 29.
314 Euphorbia Preslii - Guss. Oruzaba - July 26.
315 Euphorbia sp? Mt. O. 10,000°. Aug 6.
316 Euphorbia sp? Cordaba. 3000°. Aug 20.
317 Phyllanthus lathyroides. HBK. var genuinus
Müll - Orizaba. 4000°. July 30.
318 Croton Neo-mexicana. Müll - Mt. O. 9000° Aug 4.
319 Croton glabellus - Linn - Near Cordaba
320 Argythamnia sp? Oriz.) 3000° Aug 20.
321 Acalypha macrostachya - Jacq. " Cordaba,
3000°. Aug 20.
322 Acalypha sp? Esperanza - 8000° Aug 14.
323 Acalypha sp? Oruzaba - 4000° July 23.
324 Ricinus communis - L Common in
Orizaba - 4000°. July 23.

326 | Quercus insignis - M. &g.? Mt. O.
9 - 10,000°. Aug 7.

327 | Quercus florosa - Lieb.? Mt.O. 9-11,000° Aug. 7.

Salicineàe

328 | Salix - n sp? Maltrata 5482° - Aug. 16.

Coniferàe

329 | Pinus - sp. Mt. O. 10,000 - 14000° Aug 7.
330 | Abies religiosa - Cham &Schl. Mt. O. 12,000°. Aug 7.

Irideae

331 | Nemastylis tenuis - Benth. Rocky hill, Oriza
ba. 4000° July 31.
332 | Sisyrinchium angustifolium - Mill.
Orizaba. 4000° July 29.
333 | Sisyrinchium hartwegi - Bak.? Orizaba. July 26
334 | Sisyrinchium scabrum. Ch. &Schl? Mt. Oriz.
9000°, Aug 9.
335 | Sisyrinchium tinctorum. HBK. Esperanza.
Wooded hills 8,000° - Aug 15.

Amaryllideae

336 | Hymenocallis sp? Cordoba, 3000° - Aug 20.

Smilax sp. Cordaba. 3000° - Aug. 20.

Smilax sp². Cordaba. 3.000° - Aug 20

Yucca sp~ Esperanza, 8.000° Aug 15,

Yucca sp~ Esperanza 8000° Aug 15?

Anthericum Torreyi - Bak. First time re
          ported from S. Mex. Esperanza 8000, Aug.

Echeandia terniflora - Oth. - Very Common,
          Orizaba, Cord. & Nogales.

Allium N sp. Mt. O. 10.000° - Aug. 6.

Stenanthium frigidum Kunth - Peak of
          Orizaba. 12.000° Aug. 6.

Zygadenus? Orizaba - 4000° Aug 13.

355	Canna	sp.	Cordoba,	3000.	Aug 20
356	Canna	sp.	Cordoba	3000	Aug 21

Cyperaceàe

357	Cyperus	sp. Orizaba,	4000°	July 31
358	Cyperus	sp.	"	"	" "
359	Cyperus	sp.	"	"	" 29
360	Cyperus	sp.	"	"	" 27
361	Cyperus	sp.	..	"	" "
362	Cyperus	sp.	City of Mexico, 7000°	July 20
363	Cyperus	sp.	Peak of Orizaba, 9000° Aug 8
364	Cyperus	sp.	Orizaba, 4000°	Aug 13
365	Scirpus	sp.	Cordoba, 3000°	Aug 21.
366	Rhynchospora	sp.	Cordoba, 3000°	Aug 20.

Gramineàe

367	Paspalum	sp.	Orizaba, 4000°	July 29
368	Paspalum	sp.	"	"	" ..
369	Paspalum	sp.	"	"	.. 31.
370	Panicum	sp.	"	"	" 29
371	Panicum	sp.	Cordoba, 3000°	Aug 20

372	Panicum sp²	Esperanza	8.000°	Aug 14
373	Panicum sp²	City of Mex.	7.000°	July 20
374	Panicum sp²	Cordaba	3.000°	Aug 20
375	Panicum sp²	Peak of Orizaba	10,000°	Aug 6
376	Panicum sp²	Peak of Orizaba	9.000°	Aug 9
377	Setaria sp²	Orizaba	4.000°	July 31
378	Setaria sp²	City of Mex.	7.000°	July 20
379	Setaria sp²	Peak of Oriz.	9.000°	Aug 8.
380	Setaria sp²	Peak of Oriz.	10.000°	Aug 6
381	Cenchrus sp²	Orizaba	4.000°	July 27
382	Erianthus saccharoides. Mx.	Orizaba	4.000°	July.
383	Andropogon sp²	Nogales	4202°	Aug 13.
384	Andropogon sp²	Orizaba	4000°	July 31
385	Andropogon sp²	Orizaba	4.000°	July 31
386	Aristida sp²	Esperanza	8.000°	Aug 14
387	Aristida sp²	Peak of O.	11,000°	Aug 5
388	Aristida sp²	Peak of O.	10.000°	Aug 5
389	Stipa sp²	Cordaba	3.000°	Aug 20
390	Muehlenbergia sp²	Peak of O.	9.000°	Aug 8
391	Muehlenbergia sp²	Cordaba	3.000°	Aug 21
392	Muehlenbergia sp	City of Mex.	7000°	July 20
393	Sporabolus sp²	Orizaba	4.000°	Aug 13
394	Agrostis sp²	Peak of O.	13.000°	Aug 6.
395	Agrostis sp²	Peak of O.	12000°	Aug 6
396	Agrostis sp²	Peak of O.	9.000°	Aug 9.
397	Trisetum sp²	Peak of O.	13.000°	Aug 7
398	Bouteloua sp²	Orizaba	4.000°	July 31
399	Bouteloua sp.	Peak of O.	9.000°	Aug 8.

Eleusine sp. Common in Orizaba. 4,000° July 27

Eragrostis sp. Esperanza, 8,000° Aug 14.

Eragrostis sp. Peak of O. 9,000° Aug 9

Poa sp. Peak of O. 9,000° Aug 8.

Festuca sp. Peak of O. <u>14,000°</u>. Aug 7.

Festuca sp. Peak of O. 13,000° Aug 7.

Festuca sp. Peak of O. 10,000° Aug 6.

Elymus sp. City of M. 7,000° July 20

Bromus sp. Peak of O. 10,000° Aug 6.

Filices

Cyathea mexicana - Ch. & Schl. Wet ravines
         Orizaba. 4,000° Aug 26.

Woodsia mexicana - Fée. (Hems. includes it
     under W. mollis J.Sm.) Peak of O. 9,000° Aug 8

Cystopteris fragilis - Bernh. Peak of O. 10,000° Aug 8

Adiantum concinnum - HBK. Orizaba,
                 4,000° - July 28

Adiantum tetraphyllum. Willd - Ravines
             near Cordoba. 3,000° Aug 20.

Adiantum (near convolutum, Jaura).
                 Orizaba, 4,000°. July 31

Hypolepis repens Presl. Orizaba. 4,000° July 27

Cheilanthes alabamensis - Fée (Included under
     microphylla by Hems.) Orizaba. 4,000 July 3.

Cheilanthes - Fendleri. Hook. Peak of Orizaba
                 9,000° Aug 6.

Cheilanthes microphylla - Swz. Common
on hills near Orizaba, 4000° July 31.

Leavea cordifolia - Sag. Near Maltrata.
5482°. Aug 16

Pellaea flexuosa - Link - Orizaba - 4.000.° Aug 13

Pellaea - (Between angustifolia Bak & Park.
lyae. Bak.) Nogales - Aug 13

Pellaea - Nearest glauca J.Sm. (which Hems.
includes under marginata. Bak) Peak of O. 9000°. Aug 8

Pellaea N. Sp ? Orizaba - 4.000° July 26
(near marginata. Bak)

Pellaea marginata B. var. pyramidalis B.
Orizaba - 4.000° July 31.

Pellaea intramarginalis - J.Sm Maltrata.
5482° - Aug 15.

Pteris aquilina - L. Orizaba. 4000 Aug 13.

Pteris longifolia - L. Orizaba 4.000 Aug 13.

Pellaea rigida - HB. Orizaba 4.000. Aug 13.

Pellaea ternifolia - L. Peak of O. 9.000° Aug 5

Blechnum occidentale - L. Orizaba 4000° July 27.

Asplenium - (near cultifolium - L - wch
is not reported fr. Mex) Cordoba, 3.000° Aug 2

Asplenium firmum - Kunze. Cordoba. Aug 2

Asplenium fragrans - Swz. Cordoba. 4.000° Aug 20

Asplenium monanthum - L. Peak of Oriz.
10,000° - Aug 6.

Asplenium trichomanes - L. Peak of Orizaba
14.000° Aug 7.

436 Asplenum Shepherdi. Spreng. Cordoba,
                                    3,000° Aug 20

437 Aspidium patens. Swz. Orizaba - 4,000° Aug 13.

438 Aspidium trifoliatum - Swz. Orizaba. 4000° Aug 13

439 Nephrolepis exaltata - Schott. Orizaba. 4000° July 27.

440 Polypodium angustifolium - Swz Orizaba. 4000. A. 13.

441 Polypodium furfuraceum Schl. Common on

442   roofs of houses. Orizaba - 4,000° July 23.

443 Polypodium glaucophyllum. Kze.^ie Cordoba.
                   Cultivated. 3,000° Aug 21.

444 Polypodium lanceolatum. L. Peak of Orizaba.
                   Growing on trees - 11,500°. Aug 6.

445 Polypodium lycopodioides - L. Cordoba 3000 Aug 21

446 Polypodium pectinatum. L. Cordoba. 3,000° Aug 21

447 Polypodium phyllitidis - L. Cordoba. 3,000° Aug 21

448 Polypodium pulchrum. Mr.G. Orizaba. 4,000. July

449 Polypodium thysanolepis - Al.Br. Orizaba

450 Phegop^   4000 July 25.

451 Phegopteris rudis. Mett. Orizaba 4000° July 27.

452 Phegopteris tetragonum Swz. Cordoba 3000° Aug 20.

453 Phegopteris sp^2 Cordoba. 3,000° Aug 20

454 Notholaena ferruginea - Hk. Orizaba. 4000° July 31.

455 Notholaena sinuata. Kaulf. Oriz. 4,000° July 31.

456 Gymnogramme calomelanos. Kaulf^? (Fronds
                too large) Orizaba - 4,000°. Aug 13.

457 Gymnogramme podophylla - Tourn. (Includes
          by Hms under ehrenbergiana. Nogales.
                            4202°- Aug 13

Equisetaceae.

458 Equisetum robustum - A.Br. Along streams
near Nogales - 4302°. Aug 13.

Selaginellaceae

459 Selaginella cuspidata— spring. Orizaba -
4'   4000° - Aug 13.
460 Selaginella rupestris. Spr. Cordaba 3000° Aug 30
461 Selaginella sp?   Cordaba. 3000° Aug 20.
———? Peak of Orizaba. 13000° Aug 7.

The following list is added. ———

462 Ranunculus Hookeri - Schl. Orizaba
4000°. July 23
463 Arenaria bryoides - Willd. Peak of O. 13000' Aug 7.
464 Hibiscus Macrostus. L. (Cultivated) Cordaba, 3000°. Aug 21.
465 Malthenia Americana - L.   Along the rail
road - Nogales. Aug. 4.
666 Hiraea macroptera DC. Orizaba. 4000° July 30.
467 Rhynchosia longeracemosa. M+G. Peak. of O. 9000°. Aug 8.
467 Indigofera excelsa. M+G. Peak of O. 9000° Aug 8.
468 Trifolium sp?   Orizaba - 4000° July 29
469 Lespedeza?   Orizaba. 4000 - Aug 24
470 Cassia sp?   Peak of O. 9000° Aug 8.
471 Mimosa lindheimeri Gray, Maltrata - 5482. Aug 16

472 Desmodium psilocarpum Gray, Peak of O. 9000° Aug 8.

473 Oenothera sp? ———— Peak of O. 9000° Aug 8

474 Linum mexicanum HBK, Orizaba. 4000° July 31

475 Erigeron mucronatus - DC - Orizaba, 4000° July 29.

476 Erigeron scaposus - DC. Orizaba - 4000° July 29

477 Erigeron maximus. Otto. Orizaba, 4000 - July 31.

478 Erigeron delphinifolius. Willd? Peak of Orizaba. 9000° - Aug 8

479 Erigeron longipes. DC - Near Maltratra.

480 Baccharis rhexioides, 5482° - Aug 16. HBK - Orizaba - 4000° & City of M. 7000°

481 Aster divaricatus - Nutt. Orizaba - 4000° July 29

482 Gnaphalium leptophyllum - DC. Peak of O. 4000° - Aug 7.

483. Sanvitalia procumbens. Lam - Peak of Oriz. 9000° - Jul 1.

484 Perymenium discolor - Schrad - Orizaba, 4000° - July 31.

485 Verbesina microcephala - Benth? Orizaba - 4000° July 31

486 Spilanthes beccabunga - DC. Cordoba, 3000° - Aug 20

487 Conopsis liebmanii - Sch? Mt. O. 9000° Aug 8

488 Bidens heterophyllus. Ort. Common in Orizaba - 4000° - Aug 23.

489. Tridax trilobata. Hems. Peak of Oriza- ba, 9000° - Aug 8.

490 Parthenium tomentosum DC. Peak of
                   Orizaba 9000° Aug 8.

491 Helenium Mexicanum. HBK. Esperanza,
                       8000°. Aug 14.

492 Erechtites uncinata DC. Orizaba 4000° July 3

493 Senecio helodes. Benth. Peak of Orizaba.
                 13,000°. Aug 7

494 Senecio multidentatus. Schz. Peak of Orizaba
                 12000° - Aug 7.

495 Senecio sp². Peak of Orizaba - 14000°. Aug 7.

496 Cnicus nivalis. HBK. Peak of Orizaba
                 12000°. Aug 7.

497 Cnicus pubescens. Hemsley². Peak of
                 Orizaba - 12000° Aug 7.

498 Hieracium n. sp. near Fronovii and
                 nivopoppum.

499. Hieracium mexicanum. Less²². Peak of
                 Orizaba - 10.000° Aug 5.

18 — Plants unclassified —
517
               The collection consists of
68 Families. 154 Genera and 517 Species
distributed as follows —

	Families	Genera	Species
Phanerogams	65	137	465

www.ingramcontent.com/pod-product-compliance
Lightning Source LLC
Chambersburg PA
CBHW031221290326
41931CB00036B/1328